COPING WITH A
LEARNING DISABILITY

Audrey Borus

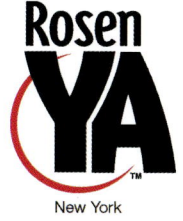

Published in 2020 by The Rosen Publishing Group, Inc.
29 East 21st Street, New York, NY 10010

Copyright © 2020 by The Rosen Publishing Group, Inc.

First Edition

All rights reserved. No part of this book may be reproduced in any form without permission in writing from the publisher, except by a reviewer.

Library of Congress Cataloging-in-Publication Data

Names: Borus, Audrey, author.
Title: Coping with a learning disability / Audrey Borus.
Description: First edition. | New York : Rosen Publishing, 2020. | Series: Coping | Includes bibliographical references and index. | Audience: Grades 7–12.
Identifiers: LCCN 2018050785| ISBN 9781508187349 (library bound) | ISBN 9781508187332 (pbk.)
Subjects: LCSH: Learning disabilities—Juvenile literature. | Learning disabled teenagers—Education—Juvenile literature.
Classification: LCC LC4704.74 .B67 2020 | DDC 371.9—dc23
LC record available at https://lccn.loc.gov/2018050785

Manufactured in China

CONTENTS

INTRODUCTION 4

CHAPTER ONE
What Are Learning Disabilities? 9

CHAPTER TWO
Types of Learning Disabilities 25

CHAPTER THREE
Reasons Behind Learning Disabilities and Other Disorders 38

CHAPTER FOUR
Getting Diagnosed 56

CHAPTER FIVE
Getting Results 70

CHAPTER SIX
Navigating to Success 86

GLOSSARY 96
FOR MORE INFORMATION 99
FOR FURTHER READING 103
BIBLIOGRAPHY 104
INDEX 109

INTRODUCTION

When he was in second grade, Dan Spencer was diagnosed with two learning disabilities. According to Spencer's essay, "Outsmarting my Disability: From Struggling Student to Conservation Educator," on the US Fish and Wildlife Pacific Region website, it was already obvious that he was "less than efficient" when it came to completing any reading or writing in class. He says he literally hid under his desk when the teacher called on him to read aloud. "And I wasn't just last to finish the test; I trailed the next to last by a solid 10 to 30 minutes. It seemed obvious to me back then that I was not only different but stupid." To make matters worse, specialists often pulled Spencer from gym to tutor him. And gym was the one place he excelled and could work off energy.

Spencer got through high school thanks to his parents and frequent academic support, and went on to college. But he was convinced he wasn't very bright. During his first year in college, Spencer says he became aware of how learning disabilities are diagnosed and what it means to have one.

Spencer realized that the difference between what he could do (his IQ) and his academic achievements

Introduction

When you have a learning disability like dyslexia, reading can often seem like an impossible task. But there are ways you can cope and go on to succeed in life!

(his grades and test scores), meant he had a learning disability. He wasn't lacking in intelligence, his brain just took in, analyzed, and communicated information differently. This made it difficult to learn by traditional methods. Soon he even realized his learning disorder (LD) could help him think in new and interesting ways that others might not consider.

School can be difficult for those with learning disabilities. But help is available. There are strategies and ways to work with a learning disability to make academics easier.

If someone had told Spencer in high school that he would earn high honors in Biology, he would have laughed. If someone had told him he'd become a conservation scientist and educator, he would have told them they were crazy. But despite academic setbacks, Spencer did those things. He was able to achieve so much in large part because he learned to

Introduction

One of the best ways to understand learning disabilities is to become informed about them. There is a great deal of information available online, from doctors and counselors, and in this resource!

view his disability differently. He was able to realize his cognitive potential.

As in Spencer's case, addressing a learning disability starts with becoming informed. Understanding how the brain works and the biological basis for learning differences is a start. According to the National Center for Education

Statistics, nearly 2.3 million public school students have been diagnosed with specific learning disabilities. Learning disabilities are a neurological condition that interferes with an individual's ability to store, process, or produce information. Learning disabilities affect a person's ability to read, write, speak, spell, compute math, and reason. Specific learning disabilities also affect attention, memory, coordination, social skills, and emotional maturity.

If you are reading this book because you have a learning disability or know someone who does, you are taking a positive step. By becoming informed and learning about available resources, you will be empowered, like Dan Spencer, to make the most of your intellectual potential.

What Are Learning Disabilities?

CHAPTER ONE

In a scholarship acceptance speech at the National Center for Learning Disabilities (NCLD), Hannah Pintado remembers:

From first grade I knew something was wrong. First grade is the year children tend to learn how to read fluently. I noticed that the other students were able to read faster than me and fly through questions. By the time I finished a story, I could not even understand what it was about. The worse part was that even though I read the passage several times, everyone thought I didn't read it and was "dumb.

For a person with a learning disability, volunteering in class can be scary and intimidating. Because those with learning disabilities process information differently, it can be hard to keep up.

Pintado was born with a learning disability that affected the way she learned to read. Her speech describes the way a lot of kids with learning disabilities feel when they are growing up: confused, alone, and not very smart (even though in many cases students with learning disabilities have above-average intelligence). Though they look the same as everyone else, they feel very different.

In a way, this is true. People with learning disabilities are different. Something in their brains makes it hard for information to flow freely. According to the National Institutes of Health's "About Learning Disabilities" web page, learning difficulties are conditions that affect how someone learns to read, write, speak, work with numbers, coordinate movement, or direct attention. Scientists believe that these difficulties are a result of differences in brain structure that affect the way someone processes information.

But finding an exact definition for the term "learning disability" is hard because no two people are exactly alike. Acquiring knowledge is a unique process for every student. Like all students, kids with learning disabilities have their own strengths and weaknesses. Some struggle with multiple areas of learning, like reading, math, and following directions, while others may have only one real learning challenge. Experts acknowledge that even though learning difficulties can be categorized, labeling doesn't necessarily make diagnosis easier.

People with learning disabilities do not outgrow them. While most people develop strategies for coping with their weaknesses and playing up their strengths, learning disabilities do not go away. The cluster of symptoms underlying your disability do not disappear as you get older, so it's important to learn how to deal with it.

The Learning Process

Before one can understand learning disabilities, one needs to understand how humans learn. Learning is a complex process. It involves an input (such as an audio or visual cue), integration (or processing), memory (the ability to remember information and use it when you need it), and output. When you study, billions of nerve cells (also called *neurons*) send electrical impulses to different portions of the brain. Hundreds of chemicals stimulate the cells to send impulses or stop them. You are born with about one hundred billion nerve cells, but most of them are not active. As you grow and take in a sound, a smell, or the way a word is spelled, your nerve cells turn on and begin sending signals to each other. This sets off a chain reaction until the information arrives at its destination or is lost along the chain. Throughout childhood, adolescence, and early adulthood, gaps that exist between the nerve cells get closed with "learning connections." When your brain receives the same sensory information later, it responds more quickly. You "learn" from experience.

Where It All Happens

Learning takes place in the cerebral cortex, the part of the brain that controls language, muscle movement, cognition (thinking), and executive functioning (the set of mental skills used to set goals, plan, and get things done). The brain has a left and right side (or hemisphere). Each hemisphere controls movement on the opposite side of the body and each plays a crucial role in different aspects of learning. The left hemisphere handles language tasks and the right dominates visual and nonverbal tasks. But the regions in the cerebral cortex don't work in isolation: they must work together for you to do something as routine as washing your face.

For a long time, researchers suspected that differences in brain structure might be the cause

Coping with a Learning Disability

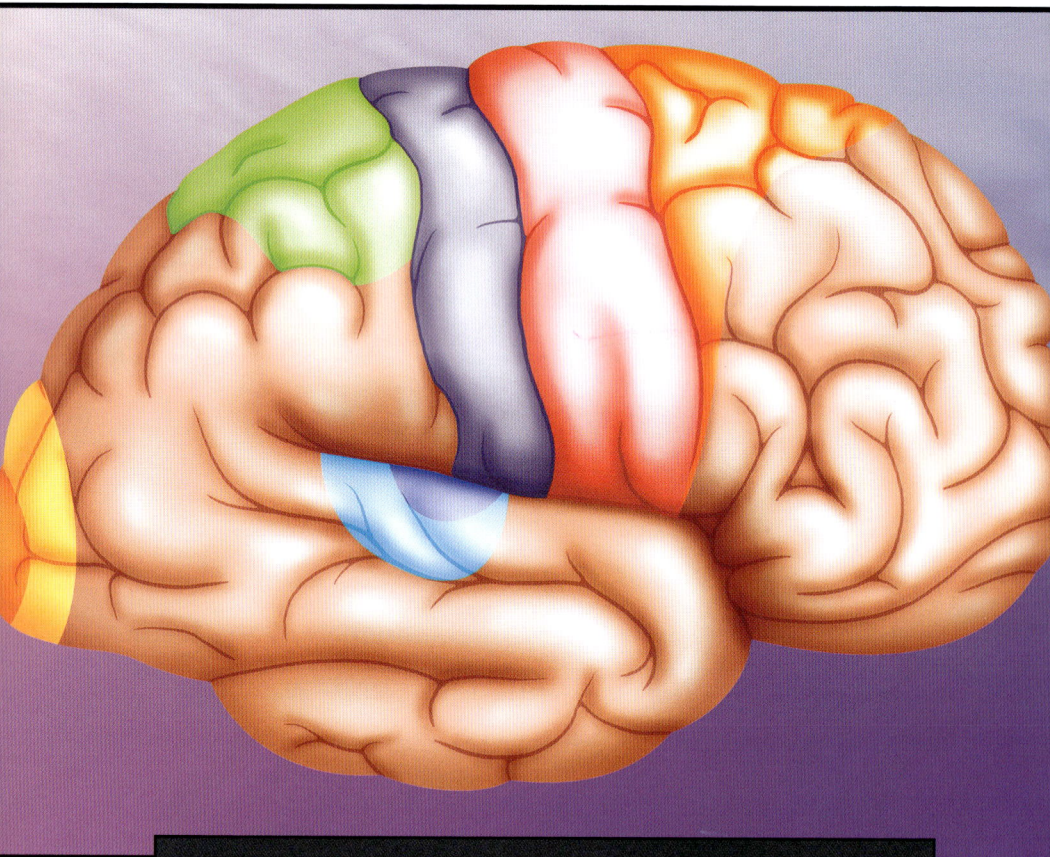

The brain is divided into different sides, or hemispheres, each of which perform different tasks. Scientists study brain scans to better understand learning disabilities.

of learning disabilities. In the 1980s, advances in magnetic resonance imaging (MRI) allowed experts to get detailed pictures of the brain in action. For example, functional MRI (or fMRI) can create images that actually show what parts of the brain are involved in reading or writing. When

Scanning for Answers

In 2013, researchers at the Massachusetts Institute of Technology (MIT) and Children's Hospital in Boston found a connection between poor prereading skills in kindergarteners and the size of a neural pathway called the arcuate fasciculus that connects the parts of the brain that control language. Ann Trafton wrote for *MIT News* that researchers found that the looser the connection between the language areas of the brain, the smaller the arcuate fasciculus.

Because the arcuate fasciculus connects those parts of the brain involved with reading, writing, grammar, sentence structure, definition, usage and pronunciation, and commits all this to language memory, the denser its fibers are, the better the command of vocabulary and language.

the brain is active, neurons consume more energy, which causes more blood to flow into it. The brain literally lights up. Using this and other technologies, research has shown that people with a learning difficulty exhibit a different activity pattern than those without. Studies also revealed differences in sizes of the two hemispheres. People who have reading disabilities often have a larger right hemisphere—the area dominant in visual tasks.

Learning Disabilities Versus Other Learning Issues

People with a learning disability are not intellectually disabled. An intellectually disabled person has limited intellectual and adaptive skills. They lack the ability to care for themselves, to live independently, and interact in socially acceptable ways. While people with learning disabilities may be weak in one area of learning, they usually have a corresponding strength in another area.

Learning disabilities do not stem from cultural differences. Children who do not speak English at home may have fewer chances to learn English when they are young. While this may limit their ability to develop an English vocabulary or present a challenge at school, it does not mean they have a learning disability.

The more you know about what is and is not a learning disability, the easier it can be to get help if you need it.

What Are Learning Disabilities?

It is important to remember that cultural differences are not learning disabilities. Speaking one language at home and another at school does not hinder aptitude—it can even help!

Ten Questions about Learning Disabilities

1. How do you "get" a learning disability?

In a word, you are born with it. According to LD OnLine, "Questions + Answers," it's important to understand that learning disabilities are not one thing, but rather the name given to a range

17

of specific disorders that create real obstacles for success in school, on the job, and in life. Remember, they have a neurological basis; that is, something inside your brain is different from that of a person who does not have the same learning disability. And determining whether you have a learning disability is a process that unfolds over time and must include information from multiple sources.

2. **Do people with a learning disability have lower IQs?**

   Nope. Those with learning disabilities are usually of average or above average intelligence. If one has a learning disorder, it is normal to have difficulty and need extra help in one or two areas. When one has a learning disability, that means that a person's skills in a one area (like reading or math) are lower than expected, based on IQ.

3. **Can learning disabilities get worse as a person ages?**

   Learning disabilities can cause new difficulties for a person as one ages. This is true particularly if someone with learning disorders changes schools or jobs. Such transitions can be stressful.

What Are Learning Disabilities?

Learning disabilities are brain based and cover a range of disorders. They can sometimes make succeeding in school challenging or difficult.

If one notices their learning disorder interfering with their life in a new way, it is okay to need extra help coping. Seeing a doctor to ensure there isn't a physical reason for new problems is also a good idea.

4. What is the difference between a person with a learning disability and a slow learner?

According to the US Department of Education, when one has a learning disorder, one has "disorders in one or more basic psychological processes involved in understanding or using language, spoken or written, which may manifest itself in an imperfect ability to listen, think, speak, read, write, spell or do mathematical calculations." However, it can be hard to tell the difference between slow learners and someone with a learning disability. Someone with a learning disability has trouble in one or two areas, and does well elsewhere.

5. How common are language-based learning disabilities?

The International Dyslexia Association and the Learning Disabilities Association of America, estimates that about 15 percent of the population (nearly one in seven) has a learning disability. For students with learning disabilities who get extra help in school, 70 to 80 percent get assistance with reading.

6. Is a learning disability a mental illness?

Nope. While certain mental issues may arise when one has a learning difficulty, learning difficulties are the result of "faulty wiring" in specific areas of the brain. These disabilities affect a person's ability to process and to use information and, thus, his or her ability to be successful with reading, writing, math, and other learning tasks.

7. Has the number of people diagnosed with a learning disability increased? It seems like everyone has one.

According to the National Center for Education Statistics, between 4 and 6 percent of the population has a learning disability. The majority of those people have trouble with reading. That number has remained constant for the last decade.

8. Aren't students with learning disabilities just lazy?

Learning disabilities are not about laziness or a lack of motivation. These are real disorders whose impacts can be felt so many ways. To get an idea of what a disability feels like, Dr. Sheldon

Horwitz of the National Center for Learning Disabilities says when talking to *PBS News Hour*, "Imagine how you would feel if every time you read something new you needed extra time to sound out each word, re-read each sentence more than once to retain its meaning, and struggle to remember details and take notes." If someone had to deal with these concerns, then also be worried about their teacher calling on them to read aloud or write on the board, it would be quite stressful.

9. How are learning disabilities different from learning preferences?

You may know people who choose to do things a certain way; for example, they are great at remembering names but never write them down. When you have a learning difficulty, your brain actually processes information differently. This does not mean that a learning disorder is a prescription for frustration or failure. Quite the opposite. But they can't just push past their differences by trying harder or being more flexible in their approach to learning.

10. Is a learning disability permanent?

Yes. There are steps you can take to get to know the way your brain works and how to best advocate for what you need. Your brain will still work differently as an adult, but you will have learned many new skills and ways of getting around your difficulties. Adults with learning disorders, who find a career where they can use their strengths and get around their difficulties, can be very successful.

Myths & FACTS

Myth: There is a specific set of symptoms associated with learning disorders.

Fact: The symptoms of learning disabilities are diverse and affect development and achievement differently. Some of the more frequently displayed symptoms are short attention span, poor memory, difficulty following directions, difficulty reading and writing, poor eye-hand coordination, and difficulty with putting things in chronological order.

Myth: Learning disorders mean you cannot learn.

Fact: What is true is that certain ways of learning may be more difficult than others. For example, if you have a reading disability the act of reading words may pose a challenge, but you can learn from audio or films.

Myth: Having a learning disorder will ruin your life.

Fact: Untrue. There are plenty of people with learning disorders who have gone on to be successful; for example, Winston Churchill, comedians Whoopi Goldberg and Jay Leno, and actor Orlando Bloom.

Types of Learning Disabilities

CHAPTER TWO

Though the term covers a lot of conditions, learning disabilities can be grouped into several main categories. You'll often hear that people with learning difficulties have brains that are "wired" differently. This is important to keep in mind. People with learning disabilities are not stupid; their brains literally work differently. Most learning disabilities fall into one of two categories: language and nonlanguage.

Language Disorders

People with language-learning disabilities have difficulty with words, both spoken and written.

People with dyslexia have trouble reading, writing, spelling, and doing math. A page of text might appear to them as only scrambled and jumbled letters, not words.

Some people with language-learning disabilities may be able to read or write just fine but struggle with other aspects of language. For example, they may be able to sound out a sentence or paragraph perfectly, making them good readers, but they can't relate to the words in ways that will allow them to make sense of what they're reading (such as forming a picture of a thing or situation). And some people have trouble with the act of writing as their brains struggle to control the many things that go into it—from moving their hand to form letter shapes to remembering the correct grammar rules involved in writing down a sentence.

Dyslexia

Dyslexia is a type of language disorder that affects a person's ability to read, write, spell, and do math. The term comes from the Greek words *dys*, meaning poor or difficulty with, and *lexis*, meaning word or language. If you have this disorder, you may read slowly and struggle to recall and decode words. You may also skip words or entire lines of text and have difficulty staying focused on material. Dyslexia is common; according to the website LD OnLine, more than 2.8 million school-aged children are currently diagnosed with dyslexia.

Because people with dyslexia tend to reverse letters in a word or read a word backwards, a common myth about the disorder is that it is linked to problems with the way your brain processes visual information. However, there is no evidence that dyslexics actually see words or letters backwards. In fact, in the early stages of learning, many kids read and write backwards.

Dyslexia makes it hard to break down words into their smallest and discreet unit of sound (called a phoneme). When one has dyslexia, one can't string phonemes together to form words because one cannot connect sounds to their written letters. Without the skill of linking sounds to written letters—phonological awareness—one can't retrieve the sounds of letters and words from memory, and without that information it's hard to figure out how to spell and say new words. For example, when a child is learning to read and sees the letters *b-a-t*, she can retrieve the sounds for those letters from memory, blend the sounds, and read the word bat. But a child with dyslexia might incorrectly associate the sound for *p* with the letter *b* and read the word as *pat*. Many of the same auditory processing skills are used in other areas of language learning—writing, spelling, memorizing vocabulary, and following verbal instructions—and people who are dyslexic may have trouble with these tasks.

Types of Learning Disabilities

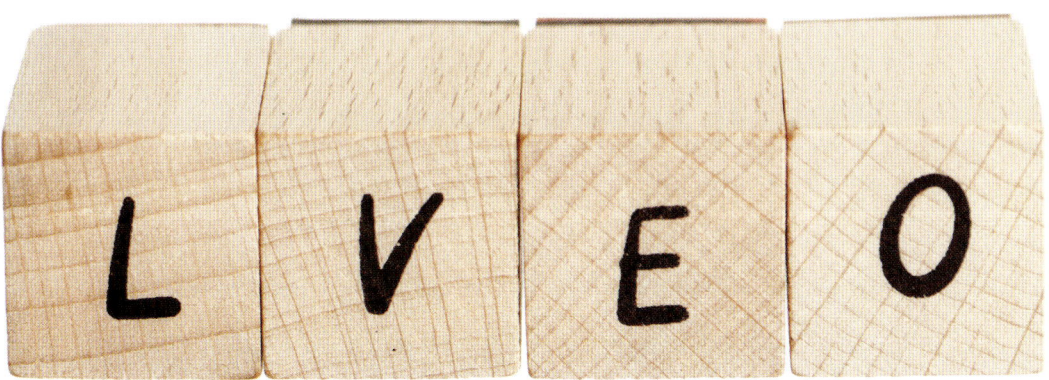

It is not uncommon for dyslexics to mix up the letters in a word. When letters are scrambled, it can be difficult to read. But there are strategies to help.

Dyslexia tends to run in families. Current research at the University of Michigan suggests that there are certain genes for dyslexia and speech-language impairment. Scientists at the university recently identified chromosomes 3, 6, and 15 as potentially related to dyslexia and language impairment.

Dysgraphia

Dysgraphia, or difficulty writing, is another language disorder often coupled with dyslexia. People with dysgraphia tend to have messy, illegible handwriting. Writing can be torture as one starts and stops, trying to figure out what letters go where because words never look the same way twice. When one has trouble sequencing and organizing auditory information, it's hard to recall the order of letters and words. There may also be a problem in the way one's brain relays messages to one's hand. People with dysgraphia often say that their hands cannot work as fast as their minds. Filling in forms with information like a name or address can be hard. One can become so preoccupied with the mechanics of writing that one forgets what one is trying to write. One might stare for hours trying to gather one's thoughts and get them on paper. In such cases, using a computer can help.

Types of Learning Disabilities

Small and Big Coordination

Your brain controls your movements and muscles. There are two major types of movement to know about when learning about learning disorders. Fine motor skills: When you learn to write, you use a group of small muscles in your dominant hand. Tasks like buttoning a shirt or coloring within the lines rely on the coordination of these small or fine muscles, also called fine motor skills. While most people don't even think about how to make their fingers move, a person with poor coordination has to focus

(continued on the next page)

People use fine motor skills, a group of small muscles in the hand, to perform detailed tasks like writing, tying a shoe, or putting together a puzzle.

(continued from the previous page)

on the movements of his fingers and hands when he writes, uses scissors, ties his shoes, or types. Gross motor skills: The coordination of larger muscle groups—the muscles that allow you to run, jump, or drive are gross motor skills. For any movement, your brain needs to communicate with your nerves and muscles to perform the action. Researchers believe that problems in the output phase of learning cause problems with fine and gross motor skills and that in turn may be the cause of dysgraphia.

Auditory Processing Disorders

Auditory processing disorders are closely related to language disorders. As sound travels through the ear it changes into an electrical impulse that the brain interprets. A person with auditory processing difficulties can't tell the differences between the sounds in words, even when those sounds are loud and clear enough to be heard. People with auditory processing disorders may also find it

Types of Learning Disabilities

With an auditory processing disorder, people may forget what is said to them, but they may be able to remember the tune and lyrics to a song perfectly.

difficult to tell where sounds are coming from, to make sense of the order of sounds, or to block out competing background noises. If one has an auditory processing problem, one will probably have difficulty remembering spoken instructions but no problems recalling how a song goes. Thoughts and ideas may come very slowly and one may have trouble explaining them to others. Like people with language disorders, one might be a poor speller or confuse words that sound similar. One may have trouble understanding figurative language (like metaphors) or miss a pun or joke because one interprets words quite literally. As you see, many of these characteristics are similar for people with other types of learning differences, particularly those with nonverbal learning issues.

Dyscalculia (Math Disorder)

A person with dyscalculia has trouble understanding numbers and retaining math facts. Like reading, mathematics requires memorizing, organizing, and interpreting symbols. If one has a math disorder, one struggles with counting, telling time, and ordering numbers. The concept of place values is hard to grasp and one may have trouble making change or recognizing patterns when using basic math. Further, just keeping numbers lined up or finishing a long division problem may cause grief.

The causes of dyscalculia are not entirely known. Some experts speculate that a person with this problem has an issue processing visual information. This makes it difficult for them to visualize numbers in relation to time, distance, or space. Others suggest that the problem is physical and that regions of the brain that support mathematical processing are not properly functioning.

Nonverbal Learning Disability (NLD)

The term "nonverbal learning disability" refers to people whose major language functions (like reading and speaking) are very good, but whose motor, visual, spatial, and social skills are much weaker. With a nonverbal learning disability, one may do well in academic subjects that require logic and memorization. But in literature and social studies, where one must "read between the lines" and write papers one may have difficulty. One may have problems with executive functioning skills like prioritizing work, controlling impulses, staying on task, and keeping organized. One may also find it hard to pick up on nonverbal cues, like someone's facial expression or body language. And one may find it hard to make friends or understand why people need their "space."

People with nonlanguage learning disabilities may have difficulty processing what they see. They may have trouble making sense of visual details, like numbers on a blackboard. Someone with a nonverbal learning disability may confuse the plus sign with the sign for division, for example. Some abstract concepts, like fractions, may be difficult to master for people with nonverbal learning disabilities.

Michael Brian Murphy, author of *NLD from the Inside Out*, writes:

> *A very hard question for us NLDers to answer is, "Why is this particular action the correct thing to do in this situation?" We often have an excellent, extensive vocabulary, and good rote memory skills, pay great attention to detail and are early readers. However, other language-based tasks are often a challenge.*

As someone diagnosed with NLD, Murphy believes it is unlike many other disabilities because it has no one specific sign. Instead, specialists use what Murphy calls "a laundry list of symptoms" to diagnose it.

Like other disabilities, researchers believe NLD is neurologically based but cannot agree on exactly what happens in the brain. For example, some experts think the issues may be caused by damage to the part of the brain that sends signals between the two hemispheres. Others think the problems are in the frontal lobe, the part of the brain that governs executive functioning skills.

There is still a lot researchers are discovering about learning disabilities. But knowing what type of learning disability may affect you can help you get answers—and get help.

CHAPTER THREE

Reasons Behind Learning Disabilities and Other Disorders

Not everyone who struggles in school has a learning disability. People learn in different ways and at different rates. When you study, you may find that information stays with you better if you read aloud. Or you may read silently and take notes. If you get a long-term assignment, you may prefer to work on it over several days—or just hours before it's due. These are just a few examples of learning styles. But they are not disorders.

Additionally, if you grew up in a bilingual household, you may have had fewer chances to build your English vocabulary. While it might have made it extremely challenging when you first entered school, you are not learning disabled.

Autism Spectrum Disorder Is Not a Learning Disability

Autism spectrum disorder (ASD) is a neurodevelopmental disorder that affects how kids process certain types of information. Many people with autism have difficulty with social interaction and communication. They may also get stuck on things like getting an answer to a question or repeating conversation about their topics of interest. While these behaviors affect learning, they are not specific learning disabilities. While limited interests, repetitive behavior, and lack of social skills are characteristics of nonverbal learning disabilities, these behaviors are related to a student's specific learning issues. For example, someone with visual processing issues might stand too close to you during a conversation because she has trouble judging distances. A person with ASD might be standing too close because she has a poor sense of personal space.

Who Has an LD (Learning Disorder)?

According to the US Department of Education, in 2015 and 2016, the percentage of students ages three to twenty-one receiving help for "specific learning disabilities" was 34 percent. This means that in a graduating class of 1,000 students, at least 340 of them have a learning disability. Learning disorders occur in all socioeconomic groups, but they are more likely to be noticed if a student has other problems, like behavior issues. Despite the large number of people with learning issues, many feel isolated and inferior. In an article by Sri Ravipati for *THE Journal*, statistics from the National Center for Learning Disabilities showed that if you have a learning disability you are three times more likely to drop out school than your non-learning disabled classmates. You are also twice as likely to be suspended. It can become a depressing cycle where you think you can't learn and so you don't want to try.

Why are learning disabilities so common? It may be that there are now better ways of diagnosing these issues. It can also be the fact that experts no longer lump learning disabilities in with other diagnoses, like autism or delayed development. Current thinking suggests that learning disabilities stem from three general causes: genetics, environment, and traumatic events.

Genetics

Learning disabilities tend to run in families. According to Jerome J. Schultz's article on LD

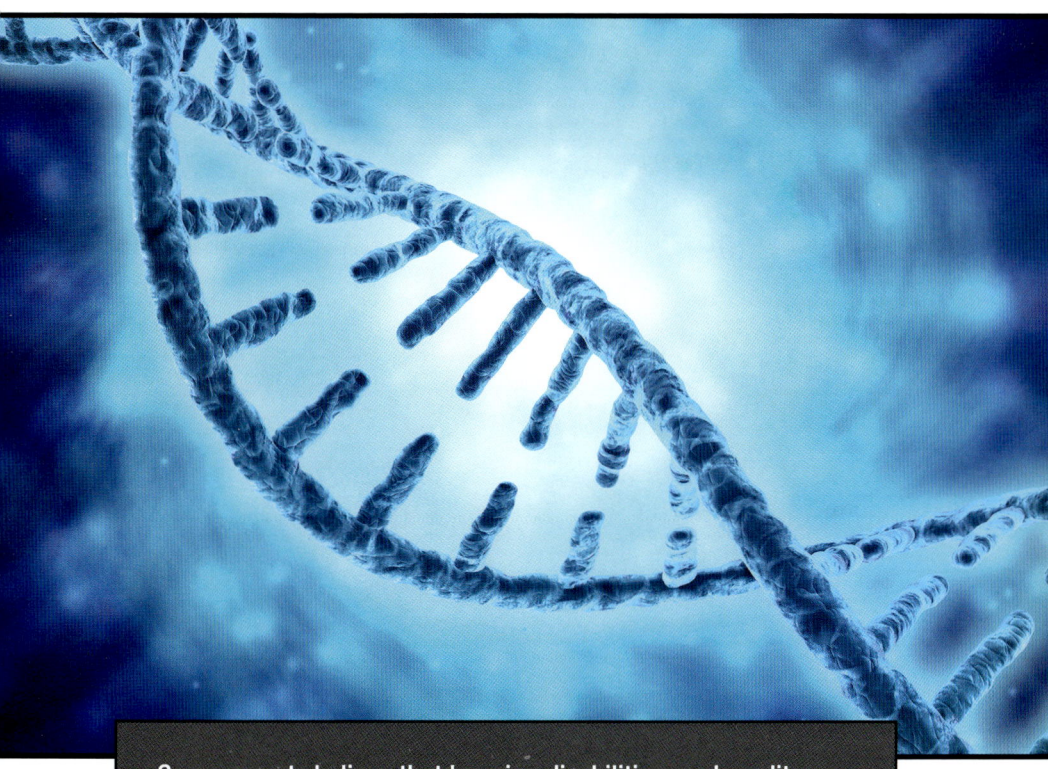

Some experts believe that learning disabilities are hereditary. They are working hard, studying DNA similar to this double helix, to try and figure it out.

OnLine, if someone in your family—a sibling or a parent—has a learning disability like dyslexia, there is a higher-than-average chance that you will, too, even though it may take a different form than your family member. Research is not conclusive, but there is evidence to suggest that people with learning disorders have experienced subtle disturbances in the way their brain structures were formed. There may be differences in cells or in the basic "hard-wiring" of their brains. As one patient put it: "my brain [has been] wired by a non-union electrician."

Environment

Another possible cause of learning disabilities is the environment, according to an article on PBS.org. Sometimes problems begin with the developing fetus. For example, if the fetus lacks oxygen or nutrition or if the mother is seriously ill or malnourished, learning disabilities may develop later. A mother who consistently drinks, uses drugs, or smokes during pregnancy is also more likely to have a learning-disabled child. Children who are born prematurely are also more prone to learning

Research has shown a connection between learning disabilities and a childhood exposure to lead paint. Lead paint was often used in older homes in the United States.

difficulties than those born full-term, especially if they are born with a very low birth weight. Further, a child whose mother has a metabolic disorder such as maternal diabetes or thyroid disease is more likely to have learning difficulties.

Babies and toddlers are especially sensitive to environmental toxins like lead, aluminum, and mercury. Lead, in particular, has been linked to learning disabilities. It is often found in older homes in pipes and paint and even low levels have a significant impact on a developing brain.

Traumatic Events

In infancy and early childhood, brains grow rapidly, alight with new learning connections. Children who experience a traumatic event like a prolonged, high fever or a head injury may be more susceptible to learning difficulties. Emotional trauma, such as seeing a parent killed or being abused may also cause learning problems. Research has shown that such events release a hormone called cortisol, which can have a damaging effect on the brain, particularly on one that is still developing. Because of trauma, it may be hard to form new memories, retain information gathered from verbal sources, or pay attention.

A parent or perceptive educator may suspect difficulties and involve others: a school psychologist or reading specialist who can observe a student in the classroom and see what's going on and how a student responds.

Signs of a Learning Disability

It's not possible to look at a person and see whether or not they have trouble learning. That may be one reason learning disabilities are so hard to diagnose, according to an article on TeensHealth. Generally, learning disabilities show up in the first years of school, when one can have trouble speaking, reading, writing, doing math, communicating, or paying attention. According to TeensHealth, "Some kids' learning disabilities are diagnosed in grade school when a parent or a teacher notices that he or she can't follow directions for a game or is struggling to do work that should be easy."

But sometimes, one can figure out ways to hide their learning issues. This is called compensation. When one compensates to cover up their learning disability, the problem isn't handled, often until person reaches adolescence. This is when school and life can get more difficult, and someone with a learning disability can begin to struggle even more. Compensating might not work anymore. Someone who has a learning disability can in silence with no one realizing they're having a problem. This is why it's important to speak up! Many people with learning disabilities realize their problem after studying hard for a test and doing poorly. Their effort is not reflected in their grade — why is this? Because their brain is working differently. Or sometimes, one can simply feel something is wrong or off. If you suspect you have a learning disorder, think about asking someone for help, like a parent or teacher.

Related Disorders

According to an article by Larry Silver for the Learning Disabilities Association of America, as many as 50 percent of people with a learning difference will also have one or more comorbid, or related, disorders. If one area of a developing brain becomes "wired differently," experts believe that other areas of the brain are affected as well. For this reason, people with a learning disability are likely to have other problems based in the cerebral cortex. Here are some of the disorders commonly associated with those who also have a learning disorder.

Language and Motor Problems

People with learning disorders often have problems processing language or may not be able to fully understand or keep up when someone is talking. Others may have no difficulty initiating a conversation but may not be able to find the right words or even organize a response when asked a question.

Another problem can be motor skills deficits, known as sensory integration disorder. People with learning disabilities and a sensory integration disorder may have difficulty coordinating teams of small muscles (fine motor skills), which makes their handwriting, buttoning, zipping, and tying difficult. Others may experience trouble coordinating teams of large muscles (gross motor skills), which makes them clumsy or unable to run easily. People with a sensory integration disorder may also have trouble coordinating eye-hand activities (like coloring) or knowing where they are in space, which makes them bump into things or knock them over.

In addition to possible language or motor difficulties, some individuals with learning difficulties may also have problems with higher-level tasks like organizing materials. They often lose, forget, or misplace things. Or they may experience difficulty analyzing a task, deciding how to address it, and then carrying it out in a timely way.

Attention-Deficit/Hyperactivity Disorder (ADHD)

Nearly half of all students with learning disabilities also have ADHD, according to LD OnLine. Children with ADHD find it extremely difficult to concentrate, pay attention, sit still, follow directions, and control impulsive behavior. While all kids are at times distractible, restless, and oblivious to parents' and teachers' instructions, students with ADHD behave this way much more often than others. Their inability to settle down, focus, and follow through on tasks makes doing what's expected, particularly at school, particularly challenging. It can also lead to conflict at home and difficulty getting along with peers.

Like learning difficulties, experts believe that ADHD is caused by a disruption in connections between neurons in the brain. ADHD also tends to

Regulating Emotions

For students with learning disabilities, anger, anxiety, and depression can be common feelings. When you feel frustrated or like a failure most of the time, it's hard to stay in control. We all experience these feelings, but for most of us the feelings are related to a specific set of circumstances or stressors.

But, for 50 percent or more of people with learning disabilities, problems regulating their emotions are not related to a situation, according to Silver's article for the Learning Disabilities Association of America. They are neurologically based and chronic, often beginning in early childhood and occurring at home, in school, and with friends.

run in families. However, unlike learning disabilities, ADHD can be treated with medication.

Anxiety

Anxiety disorders can happen in specific situations. For example, a child may experience anxiety every time his dad drops him off at school, or he may be apprehensive about social interactions, performing on stage, or being in a specific place. Or, anxiety disorders may be about life in general. Someone with anxiety problems can experience a panic attack that actually induces changes in the body: the heart rate and breathing increase, and the person may sweat and feel extremely apprehensive.

Students with learning disabilities tend to feel these symptoms more than their peers, as they feel events beyond their control are happening. When that happens, a student with a learning disability and anxiety begins to feel hopeless and freezes or panics in periods of intense pressure; for example, when taking a major test. That anxiety may cause students to miss class, tune out what's being said, and become even more disorganized.

Depression

Depression is another emotional problem that students with learning disabilities often experience. Sometimes depression comes out as irritability, decreased interest in activities, and problems

Reasons Behind Learning Disabilities and Other Disorders

In addition to a learning disability, one may have an accompanying problem like depression. If you are feeling sad or helpless, talk to an adult who can help.

sleeping. Depressed students also have trouble concentrating and making decisions. They may seem to think slowly or be tired all the time or angry at the smallest thing. If you are feeling very depressed, are having trouble getting out of bed, or are contemplating suicide, please talk with a trusted adult immediately. There are national hotlines you can call or text as well to find some help. The National Suicide Prevention Hotline, (800) 273-8255, is available twenty-four hours a day, seven days a week.

Obsessive-Compulsive Disorder

Obsessive-compulsive disorder (OCD) is a type of anxiety that haunts a person with unwanted thoughts, images, or impulses, known as obsessions, that are impossible to suppress. To diminish the anxiety, a person with this disorder develops repetitive, ritualized actions—compulsions. Common compulsive problems include the need to count or repeat behaviors, the need to check what was done over and over, the need to collect or hoard objects, the need to arrange and organize things, the need to clean and wash, or the need to bite nails or cuticles, pick at sores, or twirl or pull out hair. They are not connected in any realistic way to what the person fears. Rather, they are designed to neutralize or prevent it.

A student with both LD and OCD, Dereck Nguyen, shared on quora.com, that "it is the small, subtle things that OCD [forces] someone to do that will ultimately slow the process of learning down more than it should, with time being occupied by performing self-rituals compulsively."

Tic Disorders

A tic is a sudden, uncontrollable movement that can occur anywhere in the body. People with a motor tic disorder, such as repeated eye blinking, experience contractions of clusters of muscle. Others experience oral tics; that is, the need to say certain sounds or words. Perhaps one of the best-known tic disorders is Tourette's syndrome, a condition that includes multiple motor tics, like eye blinking, coughing, throat clearing, sniffing, or facial movements, and at least one verbal tic, like grunting or repeating a series of words. Studies have shown that while approximately 1 percent of the population has tic disorders, of that 1 percent most have learning difficulties, according to LD OnLine. Again, specific pathways in the cortex

Bipolar disorder is marked by extreme highs (called mania) and extreme lows (depression). It is a serious illness that can be treated with therapy and medication.

are suspected to be the cause, but further research must be done.

Bipolar Disorder

People with bipolar disorder can have extreme mood swings: one minute a person is unhappy while the next day, he or she can be upbeat and cheerful, unable to stop talking or sit still. Students with bipolar disorder are often unable to focus, and their energy level may wax and wane, often according to the seasons. Someone who struggles with bipolar disorder is often gifted but may have difficulty making transitions and may have other issues that make him or her distractible, inattentive, anxious, or very perfectionistic. Because people with bipolar disorder often have associated learning disabilities and an executive function deficit, they often find it challenging to organize and break things down and accomplish complex tasks.

While there are challenges that come with having a learning disorder, information can help you get help. By knowing what's wrong, you can begin to work toward a solution.

CHAPTER FOUR

Getting Diagnosed

So you, or someone in your life, think you might have a learning disorder. Here's what will happen next. Being prepared can help the process be less intimidating.

Starting Out

The first step in diagnosing a learning disability is ruling out vision or hearing problems. Once that's done, students work with a psychologist or learning specialist who uses specific tests to help diagnose the disability. Often, these can help pinpoint that person's learning strengths and weaknesses in addition to revealing a particular learning disability.

Getting Diagnosed

> By federal law, a public school must make a trained professional available to determine whether a student has learning difficulties. Usually this requires a number of tests.

Generally, learning difficulties are revealed by testing, which federal law requires public schools to administer. These tests are designed to show the difference between a student's intellectual abilities and his or her achievement. But a single test is usually not enough to make an assessment. Actual diagnosis of a learning disability can only be done by a trained professional—a clinical psychologist, educational psychologist, or sometimes a physician.

Inside an Evaluation

Say you're referred for an evaluation. What can you expect? You will be assigned a team of specialists, made up of a psychologist, a teacher trained in special education, and depending on your area of difficulty, a speech and language therapist or occupational therapist.

In most cases, your parents will first meet with the specialists, classroom teachers, and a school administrator. The purpose of the meeting is to describe your learning problems and discuss the mechanics of the evaluation: how and when you will be observed and what tests you will take. Your parents must give their permission in writing before any observations or testing can start.

IQ Tests

The psychologist will give you several types of tests. You'll get an IQ test, which measures your potential to learn and may help define a learning profile for you. Currently, IQ tests have sections that assess your verbal and nonverbal abilities. Both sections carry equal weight toward your overall score. To test your verbal abilities, you might define vocabulary, describe how words are alike, or explain concepts or social situations that require you to use practical knowledge. To test nonverbal skills, you might be asked to build a 3D structure, repeat a sequence of numbers forwards and backwards, or mentally calculate a simple math problem.

The Trouble with IQ Scores

When you're done, your team calculates an overall IQ score. The score reflects how you performed in relation to your peers, but it is often misleading. For example, if you struggle with visual tasks, your score can be below average on tests of visual memory (e.g., touching colored cards in a specific order) but in the superior range on vocabulary and verbal comprehension. Your overall IQ score would be above average but won't show your strong reading and writing skills. If you scored in the above average range for nonverbal tasks (e.g., comparing a set of pictures and determining their relationship to one another) but have trouble decoding words and reading fluently, your overall IQ score would be average. The score would show a reading disability but does not indicate that you're a nonverbal learner.

Academic Achievement Test

Another part of the evaluation is an academic achievement test. This test covers reading, writing, math, social studies, and science—more like the type of test you get in a regular classroom. This test can show how a learning disability may be affecting a student's academic performance.

All tests are supposed to occur over several days to prevent any changes in mood or focus. Once completed, the team uses the scores to determine whether you are eligible for special education services. The team looks for discrepancies in IQ and achievement and considers whether you are making academic progress, as well as how you behave in class.

A comprehensive assessment should include a combination of tests that gauge your academic

Getting Diagnosed

> An IQ test measures one's potential to learn and is used along with other tests to show the difference between intellectual abilities and achievement.

ability, information-processing capacity, attention, memory, and motor skills. The tests can be in the form of questionnaires, physical tasks, and other cognitive tests that give the evaluator a full picture of you as a learner and will ultimately help in creating a learning plan.

61

Choosing an Evaluator

Because the main evaluator (usually a psychologist) plays such an important role, that person should be someone whom you and your family are comfortable with. School districts provide evaluators, but there are also independent evaluators. Whomever you and your parents choose, the person should be accessible throughout the testing process and beyond to answer questions and provide guidance. Some questions to keep in mind are:

- What type of training does the person have? Does he or she specialize in learning and attention issues?
- What kinds of tests will he or she use? Some common tests are Scholastic Reading Inventory (SRI), Woodcock Reading Mastery Test (WRMT-II), Test of Mathematical Abilities (TOMA-3), and the Wechsler Individual Achievement Test.
- Is the evaluator a good listener? Is he or she willing to be a part of your team?
- Does he or she take the time to learn as much about your home life as your school life?

- Does he or she have a good rapport with you and your parents?
- Is he or she interested in communicating with your teachers?

Legal Implications and Rights

The US Department of Education defines a specific learning disability as "a disorder in one or more of the basic psychological processes involved in understanding or in using language, spoken or written, which disorder may manifest itself in the imperfect ability to listen, think, speak, read, write, spell, or do mathematical calculations."

"Imperfect ability" could apply to just about anyone who has ever struggled with a paper or a math problem. In many cases, a classroom teacher may be the first to notice a student with learning problems. Because second and third grade students are expected to start reading and writing with some fluency, language disabilities often surface at this time. Nonverbal and math-related problems often go unnoticed but second and third grades are often a time when these difficulties are diagnosed as students struggle to retain basic math skills.

Since the 1970s, federal and state laws have mandated that people with disabilities are entitled to "full inclusion" in all aspects of society. Section 504 of the Rehabilitation Act of 1973 made it illegal to discriminate against anyone with a disability and provided a legal avenue for those who had experienced discrimination. In 1975, Congress passed the Education for the Handicapped Act, Public Law 94-142, which is currently known as the Individuals with Disabilities Education Act (IDEA). This law ensures that all states get federal money to serve children with educational disabilities, regardless of the severity of their disability. The law states that every student must receive an "appropriate education" in the "least restrictive environment." This means that every child who has been identified with a learning disability has the right to be educated with his or her peers, as well as the right to support services from specialists at each school.

Though the 1975 changes were a remedy for years of misunderstanding and mistreatment, the reality was that many schools could not keep up with the demand for services. At that time, the government underestimated the number of children who were deemed to have learning difficulties and the cost of supporting their education. Teachers

If you are diagnosed with a learning disability, you have the right to be educated in the same classroom as your peers. You may receive support services from specialists as well.

were unprepared to teach students with learning differences. As result, a lot of students fell behind.

IDEA improved the quality of education for students with a learning disability. The law entitles every child to an evaluation by a professional team. It also allows students and their parents to have a say in decisions about classroom placement and learning. It has also opened up possibilities in the classroom. For example, special educators may teach along with the classroom teacher to give all children time in the same classroom.

While every state and district have their own procedures, federal law ensures that these steps take place:

1. **Identification.** Every school system must have a procedure for identifying students who have learning difficulties.
2. **Information gathering.** Once a student with potential learning issues has been identified, the school must have a procedure for collecting information and designing an evaluation.

3. **Evaluation.** Evaluations involving a team of specialists must take place.
4. **Conference.** Once evaluations are completed, parents/guardians must meet with school staff and specialists to review the evaluation, any diagnoses, and proposed actions, such as an individualized education program (IEP). The proceedings should be recorded in writing.
5. **Parent/guardian's decision.** Parents or guardians have the right to accept or reject any proposal. They may also request explanations or changes.
6. **Appeals.** If parents do not agree with the diagnosis, recommendations, or the IEP, they have the right to an appeals process that starts with the local school and from there, may appeal at the county or state level.
7. **Follow-up.** Each family of a public school student with learning disabilities is entitled to periodic progress reports and a formal reevaluation every three years. If parents or teachers request it, the reevaluation may take place sooner.

> One of the best ways to get support is to advocate for it. That means asking for the help you need and working hard along with adults and other allies to get it.

Response to Intervention

Even with these legal requirements, many kids with learning issues may not get the help they need. Some effectively hide their disabilities or withdraw. Others become frustrated or get by with average work and are perceived as lazy when in fact, they are underachieving because of a learning problem. Still others may be labeled as having behavior problems. Since early invention is critical, federal laws have tried to direct schools to adopt a universal screening process called Response to Intervention (RTI). Using RTI in kindergarten, teachers can step in to help children who appear to be at risk. Teachers and specialists provide instruction to struggling learners at increasing levels of intensity to accelerate their rate of learning, while closely monitoring their progress. Depending on how a student responds, teachers adjust their instruction. If a student doesn't seem to be learning, he or she will be referred for testing and evaluation. While many experts are encouraged by RTI, others feel it can only work if classroom teachers are properly trained to address a variety of academic problems and to recognize when a student actually has a learning problem and needs specialist support.

Getting an evaluation can be scary, but it is the way to get the help you may need at school.

CHAPTER FIVE

Getting Results

Let's say you've had your evaluation and what you suspected is true. You have a learning disorder. While this news can be upsetting, it can also be liberating. Now you and your family know what is wrong—and you can do something about it.

Individualized Education Program

People with learning disabilities learn to compensate. For example, to get rid of all their energy, students with ADHD might jiggle a leg or chew gum. If you know that fidgeting helps you focus, you and your parents should ask that you be allowed to use a stress ball in class or chew gum during a test. There are other accommodations that can be made to help you.

What does an IEP meeting look like? This photo is from Colorado Springs, where a mother talks with teachers about her son's education. They discussed accomodations, strategies, and more.

By law, students with a diagnosed learning disability are entitled to certain accommodations. One of these is known as an individualized education program (IEP). An IEP describes unique academic and social goals for every student who needs one. It should also outline the support (specialists and individual or group instruction) the student will get to help him or her achieve these goals. An IEP:

- Explains the student's current academic performance.
- Sets yearly goals and achievements for each area of academic weakness.
- Lists steps for achieving these goals.
- Describes specific special education and support the student will receive.
- Indicates how much the student will be in regular classes. If the student requires any special classes, the IEP must explain why.
- Estimates how long the student will require special services.
- Clarifies how the student will be evaluated to see how the plan is working.

IEP goals are important. They set the standard for how much a student should improve during an academic year. IEP goals should be SMART: specific, measurable, attainable, results-oriented, and time-bound. For example, according to the Vermont Agency of Education, an IEP that states "with the aid of a calculator, Emma will be able to solve math problems" is too general. But "with the aid of a calculator, Emma will be able to solve problems involving computation of fractions and decimals with 75 percent accuracy" is specific and measurable. It is also clear to Emma what she needs to achieve.

Traditional IEPs do not compare a student's specific goals with what other kids in his or her grade are achieving. So a student can successfully complete his IEP but still not be performing at grade level. Now some states are using standards-based IEPs. With these plans, goals are based on academic state standards. Student improvement is measured against what other kids are doing at that grade level. The purpose is to help close the achievement gap.

Ideally, an IEP should be strengths-based. This means the annual goals look at your strengths and then find ways to use those abilities to work on weaknesses. Though this approach isn't widely used yet, you and your parents can ask the IEP team to consider your strengths when setting goals.

Coping with a Learning Disability

Should I Attend My IEP Meeting?

Legally, your parents or guardians must approve any plan a team writes for you. It is also possible for you to attend the meeting. In fact, in high school, it is required. You may not have to be

Attending your IEP meeting can allow you to really tell everyone what you need to learn. Consider writing down notes ahead of time. It can help you remember and keep you calm.

present for the whole meeting. It's very common at IEP meetings for parents and staff to discuss issues that could be upsetting or embarrassing before you join the meeting. If you want to attend, you might suggest coming in when the team is planning your annual goals.

Planning and discussing annual goals can give you practice understanding your strengths and weaknesses. It also allows you to hear and discuss how the team will measure your goals. You'll have a better understanding of what is expected of you.

You may also want to talk about the accommodations the IEP has for you to be successful on tests and assignments. For example, you might know you need to have test directions read aloud or extra time to take a test. You can help give the team insights into what accommodations would work well for you.

Ultimately, whether you are part of the IEP process is a discussion you need to have with your parents or guardians. Just remember that you are capable of bringing knowledge and a fresh perspective to the meeting.

Personalized Learning Plans

Personalized learning (PL) is another approach to helping students with learning difficulties. In a nutshell, students' learning experiences (what they learn, how, when, and where) are tailored to each student, which lets him or her take ownership of the learning process. The personalized learning movement continues to grow, but the way it is implemented varies across districts, states, and organizations.

Having a personalized learning plan does not mean an IEP is unnecessary. According to the Vermont Agency of Education, personalized learning plans "articulate the learning experiences that ultimately shape a student's path to graduation, in accordance with locally-developed graduation requirements." Meanwhile, an IEP "outlines the special instruction and services needed to help a student with a disability access and progress in the general education curriculum." The Vermont Agency of Education goes on to say that these two documents complement each other, especially when it comes to assessing a student's strengths, interests, and preferences against his or her present level of performance.

Inclusion Classrooms and the Importance of Teachers

Most experts agree that students with learning difficulties and those without should be educated in the same classroom, called the inclusion classroom. Inclusion works well when the student-to-teacher ratio is low, teachers are trained to work with students of all abilities and school administrators support these efforts. In reality, many public schools in the United States can't provide this environment.

Teachers make a difference. The teachers who are most effective in supporting students with learning differences have the same qualities of good teachers everywhere. They are caring and nonjudgmental. At the same time, they have high expectations. They help students discover strengths and work on their weaknesses. If a student feels uncomfortable speaking in class, the effective teacher finds ways to

Coping with a Learning Disability

Working closely with your teacher can help you find ways to work through your learning difficulties. Help is available, though you may need to work hard to get it. You can do it!

make him or her feel heard through writing, art, or another form of expression. They allow students to take a test orally, take extra time, or provide a copy of class notes to students with learning difficulties.

Understanding Your LD

Diana is a young woman in her twenties. When she was six, she was diagnosed with ADHD, auditory processing disorder, and dyslexia. Her parents decided not to tell her until she was in high school. In an online essay for the LD OnLine website, she writes, "I was called stupid and my classmates made fun of me because I was not at their level. The principal of the school tried to kick me out because of my declining grades since he didn't want it to affect the school's reputation." Even though her parents fought for her, Diana felt stressed and inadequate. "I was jealous of the students who got straight As without even trying." Eventually, Diana understood she was just not like her peers and had to work "a million times harder to pass a class."

Despite many setbacks, Diana graduated from college and is pursuing a doctorate in biochemistry. She says in some ways she can't believe she is the same girl who used to be made fun of for being stupid. Her advice is to "never lose sight of your goals, no matter how outrageous they are because who knows … they may come true someday." She also advises not to waste time with people who put you down. "Instead try to prove them wrong and put the energy in work/school."

Assistive Technology

Without even knowing it, students who think differently develop ways to work with their learning differences. If your brain has a hard time reading pages with a lot of text, you might cover up all but a few lines so your brain doesn't get overwhelmed and you give up. This does not mean your brain is damaged. In fact, you might have a real talent for seeing the big picture when it comes to describing ideas. "While some people are better able to focus on details or the micro level of things others excel at seeing the macro version," writes entrepreneur David Flink in his book *Thinking Differently.* Flink was diagnosed with dyslexia and ADHD when he was nine.

One of the core strategies to help with learning and attention issues is assistive technology—a device or software that makes it easier to complete everyday tasks. For example, one could use an app that lets one dictate a message into a phone instead of having to type the words. Here are some other types of assistive technology that could help you learn.

Audio Players

Audio players may help you listen to words as you read. Many e-books have audio files, and smartphones and tablets come with text-to-speech software that you may find helpful. An audio recorder can capture what your teacher says in class so that you can replay it over at home.

Timers

A watch or a kitchen timer can be useful if you have problems pacing yourself. In addition to being able to see how much time you have left to complete a certain activity, using a timer can help you prepare mentally for the next thing you have to do.

Reading Guide

A reading guide is a simple type of assistive technology that people who have trouble reading find useful. The guide has a plastic strip that highlights one line of text and blocks out surrounding words that may distract you. You move the strip up and down the page as you read.

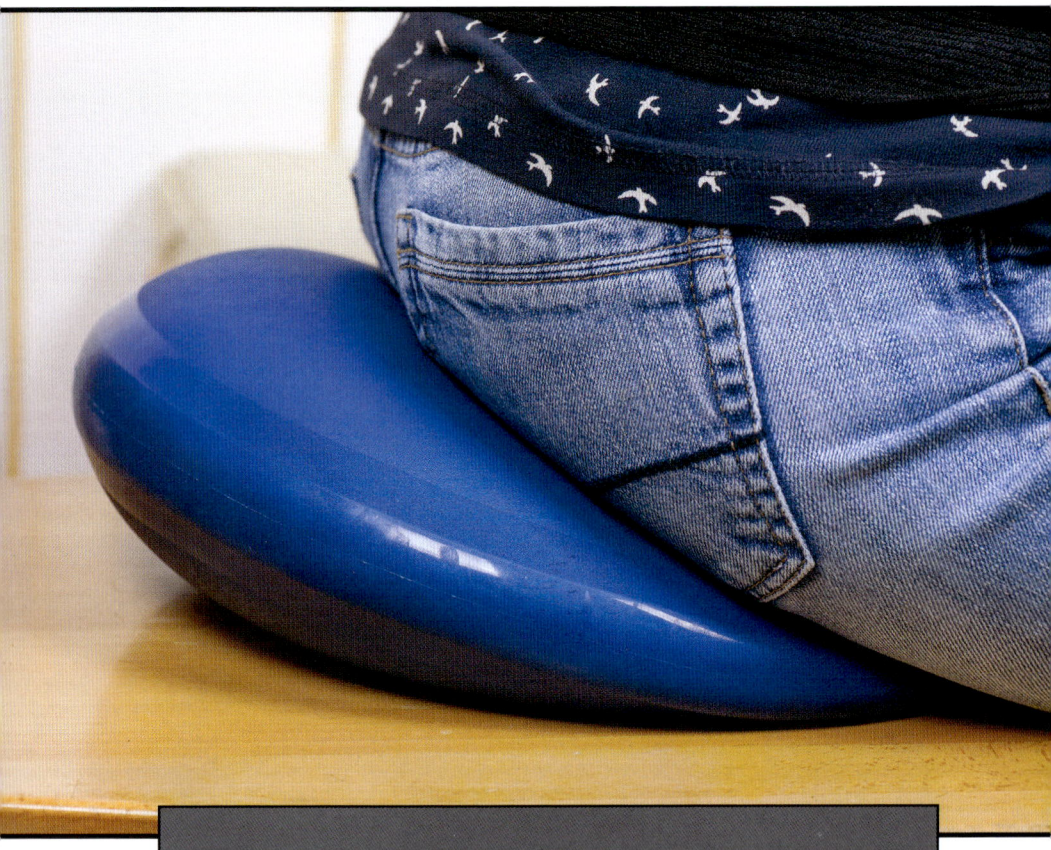

Sensory processing and attention issues can sometimes be helped by using devices such as an inflatable seat cushion, allowing for necessary stimulation and the ability to focus.

Inflatable Cushions

If you have sensory processing and attention issues, you might need to get up and walk around. But try using an inflatable seat cushion. The cushion can provide the movement and stimulation you need to maximize your focus without your having to get up.

Frequency Modulation (FM) System

Frequency modulation (FM) systems reduce distracting background noise and amplify a speaker's voice. This may help with auditory processing and attention issues. The speaker wears a microphone that broadcasts to speakers in the room or to a personal receiver. FM systems are commonly used by students with hearing impairment but also work for students who have language processing difficulties.

Calculators

Calculators can help students with dyscalculia and other math difficulties. Some calculators are equipped with built-in speech so that you can hear and confirm the numbers, symbols, and operation keys you enter.

> Sometimes, for those with dyscalculia, a calculator is the best solution for math difficulties. Technology can be a big help when it comes to learning disabilities.

Word Processors

Basic word processing can help when it comes to writing. Most come with features that check spelling and grammar. If your thoughts come quicker than you can get them down, a voice recognition system can help. Word prediction software is something else to consider: when you type the first few letters of a word, the software lists choices starting with those letters. Most of this technology is built into smartphones and tablets.

Graphic Organizers

Though not strictly "technology," graphic organizers can help you when it comes to organizing your thoughts for an assignment. You can find them online and print them or make use of online programs.

These are just a few examples of what is available. The specialists at your school will have other suggestions. There are many options to help you with your LD.

10 Great Questions to Ask a Psychologist or School Counselor About IEP Goals

1. Are they clear and understandable? Do the goals avoid jargon or undefined acronyms?

2. Are they positively worded? ("With supports, Henry will…" as opposed to "With supports, Henry will not…")

3. Do they consider how you are currently performing at school?

4. Do they address social areas that you may struggle with?

5. Do they describe how you will gain skills (e.g., identify instructional strategies)?

6. Can the goals be accomplished within the time frame of the IEP?

7. Do they include ways to measure your progress, like tests or curriculum-based measurements?

8. Is it clear what you will be able to do when you have met the goals?

9. Do they set ambitious but realistic expectations for you?

10. Do they use your strengths to help address a particular area?

CHAPTER SIX

Navigating to Success

The Frostig Center is a California-based organization whose mission is to help students with learning disabilities through consultation and research. Researchers there followed forty students from childhood to twenty years after they had graduated from high school. According to an article by Marshall Raskind and Roberta Goldberg, researchers found that there are six "success attributes" that these students share:

1. Self-awareness
2. Proactivity
3. Perseverance
4. Goal setting
5. Using support systems
6. Strong emotional coping strategies

One of those strategies is using support systems and connecting with other people. Knowing that other people share similar struggles can be a powerful experience. It can also help you remember that a learning difficulty is not a death sentence: successful people do have learning disabilities and they figure out how to get beyond them.

For example, consider Dr. Marialice B.F.X. Curran, executive director of the Digital Citizenship Institute in Glastonbury, Connecticut. Dr. Curran has been an associate professor, a middle school teacher, a principal, and a library media specialist. And she is dyslexic.

In an interview with *Forbes* magazine with Curran by Densie Brodey, Curran reveals that "[g]etting people on my team is one of the biggest secrets to my achieving my goals. It breeds positive feelings and gives me great feedback on what my talents really are." Years ago, while teaching at a local college, she authored a blog called *The Dyslexic Professor*. She wrote about her struggles with language. "There I was, alone, sending this truth out into the world and I was scared [but] it turned out to be a freeing moment.

I'd done it. I'd said the worst and nothing horrible happened. That was a huge lesson for me." It also gave her the incentive to change her career from professor to pioneering digital change in classrooms.

Curran's current work is connecting classrooms around the globe. She travels to places where she may not speak the language or know anyone, but she says her passion for her work overrides any doubts or worry about her dyslexia. "It's important to remember when you stand in front of a microphone and a giant screen to address a crowd, you know what you're talking about. That's all that matters. Nobody knows you have a disability. They are there to learn from you."

Build Your Self-Esteem

Quinn Bradlee, a filmmaker and author of *A Different Life*, a book about growing up with LDs, has made it his mission to get the word out about learning differences. He started the website www.friendsofquinn.com to give young people with learning disabilities a place where they could find resources and support.

Though at times it may be difficult, thinking about yourself in a positive way can help your self-esteem and bolster your confidence in your ability to learn.

Friends of Quinn suggests that if you have a learning difference, it may be helpful to focus on these four areas of your life: building self-esteem, organizing yourself, managing your stress, and advocating for yourself.

The way you think about yourself affects the way you see the world. When you see yourself as good, then you can work through frustrations and setbacks and feel more confident and comfortable expressing yourself. Getting praise from family, friends, and peers can help you feel worthy and respected. On the other hand, when you feel low self-esteem you lack confidence and are easily affected by what other people think. Constant criticism or being teased can make you feel worthless and forget about your strengths.

Organize!

When you have learning difficulties, it's especially important to find specific strategies to help you learn. While every student has his or her own way of studying, getting organized is one proven method for improving your learning and retaining what learn. Consider creating a quiet study environment, setting aside time to study every day, and pacing yourself. Keeping a calendar with important test and due dates and breaking working into manageable portions can help, too. When reading, break the task into sections. Consider reading part of the text and then writing a summary. This can help you find the main idea and understand the overall point of the reading. Try different strategies like these to see what works. Then you can keep what is helping you, and try different tactics if you need. Your needs might also change as you get older and the type of homework you are assigned becomes more difficult. And remember to always ask your parent or teacher for help if you need it. Together, you can succeed.

Manage Your Stress

Everyone knows what it is like to be stressed out. In biological terms, stress is the body's reaction (physical and mental) to any event that triggers a "fight or flight" response. In prehistoric times, stress could keep you from being eaten. But because you can't run out of a classroom when you get a pop quiz or argue with your teacher about not taking it, stress can build. It can make you feel anxious or frustrated, and in some cases, unable to take any action.

On the other hand, a little stress can be a good thing. Sometimes you need a burst of energy

Coping with a Learning Disability

To create an optimal learning environment, be sure to get enough sleep, exercise regularly, and eat a balanced diet. Exercising with a friend can make it fun!

for a test or a new social situation. The trick is to understand your stress and the things that "stress you out" so you can navigate through the times when you're feeling overwhelmed or more anxious than usual. Some tips for navigating stress include asking for help when you need it, getting enough sleep, exercising regularly, and eating healthy.

Advocate for Yourself

Your parents and guardians can work with teachers and other school specialists to develop a plan for your success. But as you get older, you must learn to be your own advocate. In fact, if you have an IEP in high school, part of the plan will focus on transitioning you to stand up for yourself. To get ready, here are some steps you can take right now.

1. **Know your diagnosis.** Being aware of how your brain works differently can make it easier for you to stand up for yourself.
2. **Think about future goals.** What do you want to do with your life? Do you want to go to college or will you work after high school? Are you interested in pursuing a particular career? What do you need to get there? Break down your big goals into smaller steps so you have a clear idea of where you may be going.
3. **Ask for help when you need it.** Self-advocacy means that you take initiative in solving your problems. If you find you're not keeping up in class or your grades are sliding, ask your

teachers to meet with you so you can discuss concerns and strategies.
4. **Know your strengths.** Understanding what you're good at can help you as you move toward your goals; in fact, your strengths may help you determine what you want to do in your life.
5. **Know your weaknesses.** You should also know your weaknesses. Understanding the areas of your life where you may need to pay more attention or get assistance can help you over rough spots more smoothly, and ultimately, help you achieve what you want.

Success Stories

Even though having a learning disorder can be difficult, you can still succeed. In her scholarship acceptance speech at the National Center for Learning Disabilities, Hannah Pintado said:

> LD will always cause struggle in my life. But I'm going to continue on the path I'm already walking: I've made a habit of working hard every day, and that's made it easier. I am one

Navigating to Success

LEFT: Daniel Radcliffe has a mild form of dyspraxia, a condition that makes it hard to plan and coordinate physical movement. He has never let the condition hold him back.

RIGHT: Keira Knightley was diagnosed with dyslexia when she was six. She made her parents promise that if she learned to read, they would hire her an agent.

out of many LD students who works hard to show everyone that LD doesn't have to restrain you from success in academics and life.

Here's a list of just a few people you may have heard of who have learning disabilities and have overcome them to have productive lives. You can, too!

Winston Churchill	Daniel Radcliffe
Leonardo da Vinci	Steven Spielberg
Orlando Bloom	Justin Timberlake
Keira Knightley	Tim Tebow

Glossary

accommodation A change in how a student receives instruction.

assessment The process of collecting information about a student's needs, including tests, observations, and interviews of students, family, and teachers.

assistive technology Technology that people with a learning disability use to perform tasks that would otherwise be difficult. This technology can be as simple as a reading guide or as complex as a computer that recognizes speech.

autism spectrum disorder (ASD) A range of disabilities that affect verbal and nonverbal communication and social interaction.

cerebral cortex Also known as the central cortex. The part of the brain that controls thinking and emotional functions.

cognition Thinking; the mental processes used to acquire knowledge. This includes reasoning, experience, and sense perception.

executive functions The mental processes people use to regulate their behavior and get things done. Planning, organizing, and evaluating are examples of executive functions.

fine motor skills Tasks that require use of the small muscles in the hands and fingers necessary for activities such as writing and using scissors.

gross motor skills Tasks that require use of the large muscles in the arms, legs, and torso necessary for activities like walking or running.

inclusion An approach to education in which students with learning and other disabilities spend all or most of their learning time in the classroom with students who do not have a disability. Inclusion is based on the right of all children to have access to equal education.

individualized education program (IEP) A written education plan for students ages five to twenty-two with disabilities that contains a description of the student's learning needs, goals, and objectives. The plan is developed by a team of teachers, therapists, and school administrators. It should be reviewed and updated yearly.

Individuals with Disabilities Education Act (IDEA) A federal special education law that requires public schools to serve the educational needs of all students with disabilities. To get services, a student needs an individualized education program outlining exactly what he or she needs. IDEA lays out specific requirements to ensure free appropriate education for students with disabilities in the least restrictive environment.

neurologic Of or relating to the nervous system, the group of body organs that together are responsible for various senses humans feel. Neurologic organs include ears, eyes, sensory organs of taste and smell, and sensory receptors located in muscles, skin, joints, and other parts of the body.

neuron A nerve cell. These cells receive electrochemical signals, process them, and transmit them to other cells.

phonemic awareness An understanding of how to use and manipulate the smallest unit of sound, known as phonemes, which are the foundation of all spoken and written words.

Response to Intervention (RTI) A multitier approach to the early identification and support of students with learning and behavior needs.

For More Information

Child Mind Institute
101 E. 56th Street
New York, NY 10022
(212) 308-3118
Website: http://www.childmind.org
Facebook and Instagram: @ChildMindInstitute
Twitter: @ChildMindInst

> The Child Mind Institute is a nonprofit organization dedicated to helping people struggling with mental health issues and learning disorders. This site contains an extensive library of articles on learning difficulties, along with personal stories and suggestions for how to deal with a learning disability.

Eye to Eye
50 Broad Street, Suite 1702
New York, NY 10004
(212) 537-4429
Website: https://eyetoeyenational.org
Facebook: @eyetoeyenational
Twitter: @e2enational

Eye to Eye is a national movement that offers a welcoming hand to students with learning and attention issues into a community where they can learn from near-peers who face many of the same challenges they do. The site offers mentoring opportunities as well as resources like online courses.

Learning Disabilities Association of Canada (LDAC)
20-2420 Bank Street
Ottawa, ON K1V 8S1
Canada
(613) 238-5721
Website: https://www.ldac-acta.ca
LDAC provides support and up-to-date information on learning disabilities. The site features advice from experts as well as personal stories and is subdivided into provincial chapters. Use the Find Help link to find the center in your province.

Montreal Center for Learning Disabilities
PO Box 163, Succ. NDG
Montreal, QC H4A 3P5
Canada
(514) 482-7196

For More Information

Website: http://ldmontreal.ca

Montreal Center for Learning Disabilities is a Montreal-based volunteer organization that offers support for children and adults with learning issues. They offer programs, as well as provide information on diagnosis and supports such as assistive technology.

National Center for Learning Disabilities (NCLD)
32 Laight Street, 2nd Floor
New York, NY 10013-2152
Website: https://www.ncld.org
Facebook: @NCLD.org
Twitter: @ ncldorg

NCLD seeks to transform schools and advocate for equal rights and opportunities for people with learning and attention issues. The organization is a clearinghouse for current research and support resources, and they are also involved in advocacy and working to uphold and preserve the civil rights that exist under the law for individuals with disabilities.

Understood
32 Laight Street, 1st Floor

New York, NY 10013-2152

(888) 575-7373

Website: https://www.understood.org/en

Facebook and Twitter: @Understood

Aimed at parents but written for everyone, Understood is the product of five nonprofit organizations that have joined forces to support families with LD and attention issues.

For Further Reading

Asher, Diana Harmon. *Sidetracked.* New York, NY: Amulet Books, 2017.

Beardon, Luke, and Dean Worton, eds. *Bittersweet on the Autism Spectrum.* London, England: Jessica Kingsley Publishers, 2017.

Creedle, Laura. *The Love Letters of Abelard and Lily.* Boston, MA: Houghton Mifflin Harcourt, 2017.

Dionne, Erin. *Lights, Camera, Disaster.* New York, NY: Arthur A. Levine Books, 2018.

Fenn, Jennifer. *Flight Risk: A Novel.* New York, NY: Roaring Brook Press, 2017.

Landau, Jennifer, ed. *Teens Talk About Learning Disabilities and Differences.* New York: NY, Rosen Publishing Group, 2018.

Priemaza, Anna. *Kat and Meg Conquer the World.* New York, NY: Harper Teen, 2017.

Russel, Alexei Maxim. *Trueman Bradley: Aspie Detective.* London, England: Jessica Kinglsey Publishers, 2011.

Weeks, Sarah, and Gita Varadarajan. *Save Me a Seat.* New York, NY: Scholastic Inc., 2018.

West, Thomas. *Seeing What Others Cannot See: The Hidden Advantages of Visual Thinkers and Differently Wired Brains.* Amherst, NY: Prometheus Books, 2017.

Bibliography

Brodey, Denise. "How People with Learning Disabilities Handle Their Differences in the Workplace." *Forbes*, April 22, 2018. https://www.forbes.com/sites/denisebrodey/2018/04/22/how-people-with-learning-disabilities-handle-their-differences-in-the-workplace/#5fe5bf331ec4.

Cohen, Cole, *Head Case: My Brain and Other Wonders*. New York, NY: Henry Holt and Company, 2015.

Diana. "Diana's Battle with LDs." LD OnLine, September 20, 2018. http://www.ldonline.org/firstperson/Diana%27s_battle_with_LDs.

Ehmke, Rachel. "Supporting the Emotional Needs of Kids With Learning Disabilities." Child Mind Institute, October 2, 2018. https://childmind.org/article/supporting-the-emotional-needs-of-kids-with-disabilities.

Flink, David. *Thinking Differently*. New York, NY: William Morrow, 2014.

Friends of Quinn. "For Young Adults." September 19, 2018. http://www.friendsofquinn.com/for-young-adults.

Horwitz, Sheldon. "Five Misconceptions about Learning Disabilities." *PBS News Hour*, March 16, 2012. https://www.pbs.org/newshour/health

Bibliography

/five-misconceptions-about-learning-disabilities.

Hudson, Roxanne F., Leslie High, and Stephanie Al Otaiba. "Dyslexia and the Brain: What Does Current Research Tell Us?" Retrieved August 10, 2018. http://www.ldonline.org/article/14907.

Individuals with Disabilities Act. "Chapter 33 – EDUCATION OF INDIVIDUALS WITH DISABILITIES." September 5, 2018. http://uscode.house.gov/view.xhtml?path=/prelim@title20/chapter33&edition=prelim.

Landau, Jennifer, ed. *Teens Talk about Learning Disabilities and Differences.* New York, NY: Rosen Publishing Group, 2018.

LD OnLine. "Questions + Answers: About Learning Disabilities." Retrieved November 27, 2018. http://www.ldonline.org/questions/aboutld.

Lerner, Janet W., and Beverly H. Jones. *Learning Disabilities and Related Disabilities: Strategies for Success.* 13th ed. Stamford, CT: Cengage Learning, 2015.

Murphy, Michael Brian. *NLD from the Inside Out.* 3rd ed. London, UK: Jessica Kingsley Publishers, 2016.

National Institutes of Health. "About Learning Disabilities." September 11, 2018. https://www.nichd.nih.gov/health/topics/learning/conditioninfo/default.

Nguyen, Dereck. "Is OCD a Learning Disability? If So, Why?" Quora, November 3, 2018. https://www.quora.com/Is-OCD-a-learning-disability-If-so-why.

PBSparents. "Causes of Learning Disabilities." Retrieved September 15, 2018. http://www.pbs.org/parents/education/learning-disabilities/basics/causes.

Pintado, Hannah. "Personal Statement." 2014 Anne Ford Scholarship Winner. National Center for Learning Disabilities. Retrieved September 15, 2018. https://www.ncld.org/archives/blog/2014-anne-ford-scholar-essay.

Raskind, Marshall, and Roberta Goldberg, et al. "Teaching Life Success to Students with LD: Lessons Learned from a 20 Year Study." *Intervention in School and Clinic.* Vol. 37, No. 4, March, 2002. http://frostig.org/wp-content/uploads/2015/09/Teaching-Life-Success-2002-Raskind-et-al.pdf.

Bibliography

Ravipati, Syri. "Report: Students with Learning and Attention Issues Three Times More Likely to Drop Out." *THE Journal*, May 5, 2017. https://thejournal.com/articles/2017/05/17/students-with-learning-and-attention-issues-three-times-more-likely-to-drop-out.aspx.

Regents of the University of Michigan. "Exciting Times in Dyslexia Research." Retrieved September 5, 2018. http://dyslexiahelp.umich.edu/latest/exciting-times-in-dyslexia-research.

Rodis, Pino, et al. *Learning Disabilities & Life Stories*. Boston, MA: Allyn and Bacon, 2001.

Schultz, Jerome J. "Is Dyslexia Hereditary?" LD OnLine. 2008. http://www.ldonline.org/article/27446.

Silver, Larry. "Related Disorders of a Learning Disability: What You Should Know." Retrieved September 5, 2018. http://ldaamerica.org/what-you-should-know-about-related-disorders-of-learning-disability.

Spencer, Dan. "Outsmarting My Disability: From Struggling Student to Conservation Educator." US Fishery and Wildlife Service. Retrieved September 21, 2018. http://usfwspacific.tumblr

.com/post/98738774305/outsmarting-my-disability-from-struggling-student.

TeensHealth from Nemours. "Learning Disabilities." Retrieved November 27, 2018. https://kidshealth.org/en/teens/learning-disabilities.html.

Trafton, Ann. "Brain Scans May Help Diagnose Dyslexia." *MIT News*, August 13, 2013. https://news.mit.edu/2013/brain-scans-may-help-diagnose-dyslexia-0813.

US Department of Education, National Center for Education Statistics. "Children and Youth with Disabilities." April, 2018. https://nces.ed.gov/programs/coe/indicator_cgg.asp.

Vermont Education Agency. "The Relationship Between Individualized Education Programs (IEPs), Personalized Learning Plans (PLPs), and Proficiency-Based Graduation Requirements (PBGRs)." August 15, 2016. http://education.vermont.gov/sites/aoe/files/documents/edu-proficiency-based-education-the-relationship-between-IEP-PLP-PBGR.pdf.

Index

A
accommodation, 70–72, 75
adolescence, 13, 45–46
anxiety, 49–50, 52, 55, 91–92
assessment, 57–58, 60–61
assistive technology, 80–84
attention-deficit/hyperactivity disorder (ADHD), 48–49, 70, 79, 80
auditory processing, and disorder, 28, 30, 32–34, 79, 83

B
brain
 cerebral cortex, 13–16, 46, 53, 55
 cognition, 7, 13, 61
 coordination, 8, 24, 31–32, 47
 executive functioning, 13, 35–37, 55
 hemisphere, 13–16, 37
 information and, 5, 11–13, 21–23, 28, 44, 61
 language, 13, 15, 20, 25–30, 32–36, 47–48, 63–64, 87–88
 neurologic issues, 7–8, 18, 37, 49
 neuron, 12–13, 15, 48–49
 structure, 11, 13–14, 42
 "wiring," 21, 25, 42, 46

D
diagnosis, 11, 56–69, 93
dyscalculia, 34–35, 83
dyslexia, 20, 27–30, 42, 79, 80, 87–88

E
emotions, 49–52, 86
environment, 41, 42–44, 64, 77, 90
evaluation, 58–67, 69, 70

F

fine motor skills, 31–32, 47–48

G

goals, 13, 71–73, 75, 79, 85, 86–87, 93–94
gross motor skills, 32, 47–48

I

imperfect ability, 20, 63–64
inclusion, 64, 77–78
individualized education program (IEP), 67, 70–75, 76–77, 85, 93
Individuals with Disabilities Education Act (IDEA), 64–67
information gathering, 44, 66
intelligence quotient (IQ), 4, 18, 58–60

L

language disorder, 25–27, 30, 32, 34, 47–48
Learning Disabilities Association of America, 20, 46, 49
learning disability
defined, 9–23
education plans, 70–79, 85
reasons behind, and related disorders, 38–55
statistics about, 7–8, 20–21, 27, 40, 46
success attributes, 86–88
types of, 25–37
well-known people and, 24, 95
learning disorder (LD), 5, 18–20, 22–24, 31, 40, 42, 46–47, 53, 55, 56, 70, 79, 94
legal implications, and

Index

rights, 63–67

M
memory, 8, 12, 15, 24, 28, 36, 59, 61

N
National Center for Learning Disabilities (NCLD), 9, 22, 40, 94
nonlanguage disorders, 25, 36
nonverbal learning disability (NLD), 34, 35–37, 39, 49, 59, 64
tasks, 13, 59–60

O
organizing skill, 30, 34, 36, 47–48, 55, 84, 89–91

P
parent, and/or guardian, and ADHD, 42, 48, 70, 79

meeting with specialists, 58, 62–63, 66–67, 73–75, 93
support, 4, 44–46, 79, 91
psychologist, 44, 56, 58–59, 62, 85

S
school specialist, 4, 44, 56, 64, 69, 71, 84, 93
self-advocacy, 23, 89–90, 93–94
self-esteem, 88–90
social interaction, 16, 50, 59, 85, 92
social skills, 8, 35, 39, 71
special education, 58, 60, 72
stress, 19, 22, 49, 70, 79, 89, 91–92

T
testing, 57–58, 62, 69
trauma, 41, 44

About the Author

Audrey Borus spent ten years as a school librarian instructing children with learning disabilities. She now teaches ESL at the International Institute of New England and provides reference services for students at MassBay Community College. Borus lives and works in Massachusetts and is the parent to a young adult with an LD who is applying to medical school.

Photo Credits

Cover Yulia Grigoryeva/Shutterstock.com; p. 5 © iStockphoto.com/princessdlaf; p. 6 Sergey Novikov/Shutterstock.com; p. 7 LightField Studios/Shutterstock.com; p. 10 michaeljung/Shutterstock.com; p. 14 BSIP/Universal Images Group/Getty Images; pp. 17, 65 Monkey Business Images/Shutterstock.com; p. 19 Lisa F. Young/Shutterstock.com; p. 26 © iStockphoto.com/Osvaldo Maldonado; p. 29 Swellphotography/Shutterstock.com; p. 31 Blend Images - JGI/Jamie Grill/Getty Images; p. 33 Ollyy/Shutterstock.com; p. 41 paulista/Shutterstock.com; p. 43 KMcNamara/Shutterstock.com; pp. 51, 68 pixelheadphoto digitalskillet/Shutterstock.com; p. 54 Minerva Studio/Shutterstock.com; p. 57 New Africa/Shutterstock.com; p. 61 © iStockphoto.com/KLH49; p. 71 Joe Amon/Denver Post/Getty Images; p. 74 Photographee.eu/Shutterstock.com; p. 78 asiseeit/E+/Getty Images; p. 82 Jan Schneckenhaus/Shutterstock.com; p. 83 Aiolos Design/Shutterstock.com; p. 89 cheapbooks/Shutterstock.com; p. 92 Jacek Chabraszewski/Shutterstock.com; p. 95 (top) Jason Merritt/Getty Images; p. 95 (bottom) Anthony Harvey/Getty Images.

Design and Layout: Nicole Russo-Duca; Editor: Elissa Petruzzi; Photo Researcher: Bruce Donnola